CONTENTS

Tool cupboard (top left), wine rack (far left) and storage box (left)

Plate rack

Racks made of dowelling and dowelled joints are the basis of this wall-mounted plate rack, which can be used to dry and store up to twenty-four plates.

PREPARING RAILS AND DOWELS

1 Measure all the parts and cut them to length.

2 Take the three rails. Choose the best face of each, and mark a centre line along this face with a combination square. On one rail (this will be the centre rail) mark a centre line on the next face around (not the opposite face). Mark the left-hand end of each piece to ensure they remain correctly oriented. Decide which rail will be the front rail and which the back rail and mark them.

MATERIALS*			
PART	MATERIAL	LENGTH	NO.
Rails	32 x 32 mm timber PAR	720 mm	3
Bottom runners	32 x 16 mm timber PAR	320 mm	2
Uprights	32 x 16 mm timber PAR	240 mm	2

OTHER: Five 2.4 m lengths of 8 mm dowelling; abrasive paper: fine and medium; medium and coarse sanding belts (optional); PVA adhesive (or two-part adhesive for a stronger job); 8 mm dowel jointing kit; finish of choice; two 75–100 mm (3–4 in) x No.10 gauge screws

* Finished size: 745 mm long and 320 mm deep. For a note on timber types and sizes see page 57. Timber sizes given are nominal.

TOOLS

- Pencil
- Tape
- Steel rule (600 mm)
- Combination square
- Tenon saw
- Jigsaw
- Scribe/point marker

- Electric drill
- Drill bit: 5 mm high speed steel (HSS)
- Countersink bit
- Drill stand (optional)
- Belt sander (optional)
- Cork sanding block
- Rubber mallet

- Plane (block or smoothing)
- Four sash cramps
- Scraper
- Dust mask
- Safety goggles
- Hearing protection

Made from oak with a gloss varnish finish, this plate rack makes an elegant addition to the kitchen.

Starting from the end that is marked, measure 30 mm increments along each centre line. Each rail should have twenty-three holes.

3 Use a scribe or point marker to indent each mark (this will help position the drill accurately). Using an electric drill with an 8 mm dowelling bit, bore all the holes to a depth of 10 mm, using a depth gauge (see the box on page 8). Keep checking as the depth gauge can move quite easily. It is very important to keep the drill straight. Use a drill stand if you have one available, as it will ensure the holes are straight.

4 Sand the lengths of dowel with fine abrasive paper before you cut them. Cut twenty-three lengths of dowel 205 mm long and twenty-three 225 mm long. The best way to do this is to bundle the five lengths of dowel tightly together, securing them with thick rubber bands. Measure and mark the distance to be cut and slide the rubber band just behind the mark; use a jigsaw or fine handsaw to cut the lengths. Remove

the sharp edges from the ends, either with the belt sander or hand-held abrasive paper (medium), to help the dowels fit into the holes.

5 Sand the three rails with fine abrasive paper and take the sharp corners off the long edges with a plane or cork block covered with abrasive paper. Leave the ends square. Dust off the dowels, rails and holes in the rails. Blow them out if necessary to remove all the dust.

ASSEMBLING THE RACK

6 Using a small stick shaped to suit the hole, put a small amount of adhesive in the holes of the back rail and the corresponding row of holes in the centre rail. Place dowels in the holes on one rail and, using a rubber mallet, hammer them in enough to hold them in the holes. If they are a little uneven it does not matter. With all the dowels pointing up, bring the opposing rail down onto the dowels, work them into the holes and tap with the rubber mallet. Keep working the dowels in as you tap until all the dowels are in the holes.

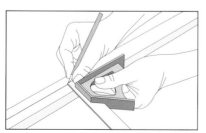

2 Use a combination square to mark a centre line down each rail and then mark off 30 mm increments along it.

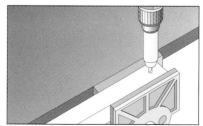

3 Using an electric drill with an 8 mm dowelling bit and a depth gauge, drill the holes for the dowels.

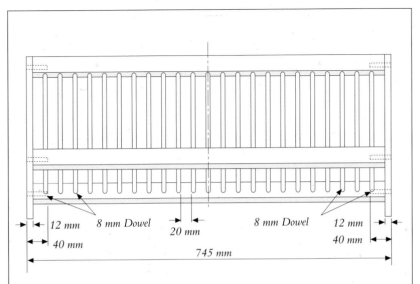

12 mm   8 mm Dowel   20 mm   8 mm Dowel   12 mm

40 mm   40 mm

745 mm

FRONT VIEW

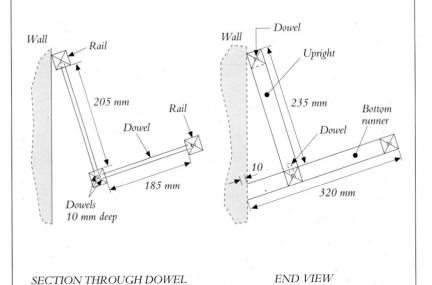

Wall   Rail

205 mm

Rail

Dowel

Dowels
10 mm deep

185 mm

Wall   Dowel

Upright

235 mm

Dowel   Bottom
runner

10

320 mm

SECTION THROUGH DOWEL   END VIEW

The bottom runners hold the rack out from the wall at an angle.

7 Use a sash cramp at each end and another two cramps in the middle to pull the two rails together and prevent bowing. It is very important to check for parallel and, using a square, make sure the dowels are square to the rails. Clean up any excess adhesive with a scraper and warm, damp rag: there should not be too much oozing out. When the adhesive is dry, remove the cramps and repeat the process on the other side.

MAKING A DEPTH GAUGE

You can make a depth gauge from a piece of 25 mm dowel. Once the drill bit is in the drill, measure the length of the bit and subtract the depth of the hole. Cut a piece of dowel to this length, place it in the vice and bore an 8 mm hole right through. Place the dowel over the drill bit, making it look like a pencil with the drill bit as the lead.

8 Take the two bottom runners. On the end that will butt up to the wall, measure in 10 mm from the end and mark across the top of the runner. Cut or plane an angle from the mark to the bottom corner.

9 Drill an 8 mm hole in the end of each rail to a depth of 30 mm. Put the centre markers from the dowel jointing kit into the holes and transfer the marks to the two bottom runners. Drill an 8 mm hole at each point, to a depth of 10 mm. Cut the dowels to 18 mm (always cut the dowel a couple of millimetres shorter than the depth of both holes added together). Check the fit with the dowels in and the bottom runners on.

10 Hold the timber for the uprights in position on the runners and mark the required length. Cut the uprights to length. Drill a hole 10 mm deep in the bottom runner, in the centre of where the upright meets it. Using the centre marker in this hole, position the upright and transfer the mark. Remove the centre marker and, placing it in the hole in the end

10 Hold the upright in position on the bottom runner and against the back rail, and mark off its length.

of the back rail, position the upright to transfer the mark. Drill the holes to 10 mm deep.

11 Check the fit of the pieces before pulling them apart. Apply the adhesive. Insert the dowels. Cramp up using sash cramps, and clean off the excess adhesive.

FINISHING

12 Sand all the glued joints. If you are using a belt sander, use a medium to fine grade belt. Keep the belt sander level, otherwise it will dig in on the edge and cause damage to the rack. With an orbital sander continue through the grades, medium to fine, on the rails and runners. Hand sand all the dowels, and apply the finish of your choice.

13 To fasten the rack to a concrete or brick wall, drill a hole about 100 mm from each end of the back rail, with a 5 mm HSS drill bit. Use 75 or 100 mm (3 or 4 in) x No.10 gauge screws, and countersink to suit the screw head. Drill the wall for wall plugs. On a stud (timber) wall first find the studs to fasten into. This will determine the positions for the screws.

MAKING JOINTS

Joining timbers and board materials is a basic requirement for carpentry, and the most effective joints are rebates and housing joints (see page 64). The quickest and most accurate way to make them is with a router. However, if you do not have a router, these joints can be made using other tools.

The joints were originally made using hand tools, some of which were very specialised. For example, rebate planes were used to make rebates. They can still be found, but they can be expensive for such a specialised tool.

Housing joints can be made with a tenon or circular saw and a chisel.

1 Mark out the position of the joints on the material. Continue markings down the edges only to the depth of the joint. Trace the lines with a trimming knife.

2 If you are using a circular saw, set the depth of the cut accurately on the saw, and cramp a batten across the board to guide the saw through the joint.

3 Saw across the face of the material twice, being careful to cut on the waste side of the lines.

4 Use the appropriate size of chisel to remove the waste until the bottom of the housing is flat and to the correct depth.

Rebates can be made using a tenon or circular saw to make a cut on each edge, and are then cleaned up with a chisel.

This practical knife rack is fixed to the wall with four screws. They can be covered with timber plugs if desired, as were the two bottom screws here.

Knife rack

Mounted on a backing board pieced together for decorative effect, this knife rack has a narrowing slot to accommodate a full range of knives as well as a place for a sharpening steel.

MAKING THE BACKBOARD

1 Measure all the parts and cut them to size, being careful to cut square and straight.

2 Take the two backboard pieces and choose which edges to join by putting them together in different ways until you see which edges fit best. Mark any high spots on the edges, and then carefully plane them away where necessary, until you achieve a satisfactory fit. Use a steel rule or straight-edge to double check

---

MATERIALS★

Part	Material	Length	No.
Backboard bottom	250 x 32 mm timber PAR	600 mm	1
Backboard top	150 x 32 mm timber PAR	600 mm	1
End pieces	50 x 32 mm timber	380 mm	2
Runners	22 x 16 mm timber	680 mm	2

OTHER: PVA adhesive; sheets of glossy plastic; 8 mm dowel jointing kit; abrasive paper: medium to fine; fine, medium and coarse sanding belts (optional); 6 mm dowel jointing kit; finish of choice

★ Finished size: 375 mm high and 680 mm wide. For a note on timber types and sizes see the box on page 57. Timber sizes given are nominal.

TOOLS

- Pencil
- Tape measure
- Steel rule (600 mm) or straight-edge
- Tenon saw
- Jigsaw
- Plane
- Two sash cramps

- Four G-cramps
- Scraper
- Belt sander (optional)
- Large square
- Chisel (sharp)
- Compasses
- Vice
- Electric drill

- Drill bit: 8.5 mm high speed steel (HSS); 15 mm speed bit
- Orbital sander
- Cork sanding block
- Round file
- Plug cutter: 10 mm
- Combination drill bit

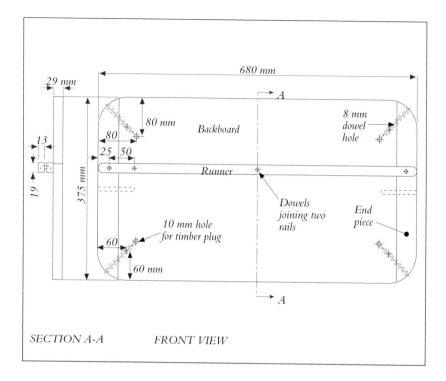

680 mm

29 mm

A

8 mm
dowel
hole

80 mm

Backboard

13

80

25 50

375 mm

19

Runner

Dowels
joining two
rails

End
piece

10 mm hole
for timber plug

60

60 mm

SECTION A-A   FRONT VIEW

that the faces of the pieces are absolutely flat.

3 Adjust two sash cramps to hold the timber, and have two G-cramps handy. You also need four scraps of timber (at least 550 mm long), to hold the timber in line as the sash cramps pull them together. Apply adhesive to the edge being glued. Do not overtighten the cramps: a firm pressure is enough. Use glossy plastic as a membrane to prevent the cramps or scrap timber adhering to the

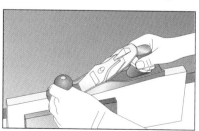

2 Take the two backboard pieces and plane the joining edges until they are completely flat.

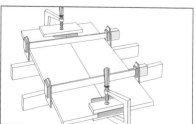

3 Use scraps of timber and small sheets of glossy plastic to protect the timber in the cramps.

project. Clean away excess adhesive with the scraper. Allow to dry.

4 Remove the cramps and plastic. Cramp or nail a thin piece of timber to the bench to stop the piece moving while you are sanding. Sand both sides, first the joint and then the faces. Use medium abrasive paper or use a coarse or medium belt in a belt sander, depending on how imperfect the joint is.

5 Choose the best face for the front, and mark the back. Using the large square, mark a pencil line down each of the short sides. Score the pencil line with a sharp chisel, using a steel rule or straight-edge as a guide. Cramp a straight batten to the timber to guide the jigsaw and cut right next to the chisel groove. Do not cut inside the groove, but very close to it on the outside—this is called 'leaving the line on' and stops the timber from lifting when you saw the edge.

6 Take the two 380 mm long pieces and fit, mark and sand, using the same method as before. Make sure

5 Use a sharp chisel and steel rule or straight-edge to cut a groove down the ends of the backboard.

the plane is very sharp, and work in from each side of the end grain to prevent the timber splitting away on the corner. Using the same method as before, glue the end pieces onto the board. Once the adhesive is dry, remove the cramps and use medium abrasive paper to sand both faces flush, using the belt sander if you have one. Sanding across the grain is unavoidable, but by working your way through the grades any marks will be removed.

7 To round off the corners of the board, turn it over so the back is facing upwards. Draw a right angle in each corner, 60 mm in from and parallel to the edges. Set the compasses at 60 mm, place the point of the compasses on the inside corner of the square and draw a radius around the outside edge of the square. Also draw a line from each board corner to the inside corner of the square, to be used later for drill direction. Using the jigsaw, cut the four radiuses. Place the piece in the vice and sand all the way round, using medium abrasive paper or the belt sander with a fine belt if you have one. Pay special attention to the rounded corners: remove saw cuts and sand them smooth and round.

INSERTING THE DOWELS
8 Dowels are inserted through the edge pieces to lock the board together, one in the middle of each rounded corner and one in the middle of each end. Mark a short

line in the centre of the edge at each position and place the board in the vice. Using the lines marked from the corners as a guide for the angle, drill holes 75 mm deep with an 8 mm dowelling bit. If the dowels are tight, re-bore the holes with an 8.5 mm HSS bit, to give the dowel a little bit of clearance.

9 Cut six 8 mm dowels 75 mm in length, and cut a slot down the centre of each, about a third of the length. Cut wedges from a small scrap of timber—they need to be 8 mm wide, about 25 mm long and 5 mm at the thick end of the wedge. Using a piece of 6 mm dowel, work adhesive down to the bottom of the hole. Apply adhesive to the dowel and wedge, and insert the wedge about halfway into the slot. Push the dowel into the hole and use a small piece of timber to tap it almost flush with the board, then tap the wedge in. Let the adhesive dry, saw off any protruding dowel and wedge, and sand smooth. Sand the face and edges with the sander, working through the grits from medium to fine.

ADDING THE RUNNERS

10 Take the runners and round the ends with the jigsaw (a small coin makes a good template). Sand the ends smooth and round, and sand the faces and edges. Decide on the front face of each piece and mark the back.

11 To make the hole for the steel, place the runners in the vice, and measure in 50 mm from one end and 14 mm from the edge. (Vary the position as necessary to fit your steel.) Using a 15 mm speed bit, drill the hole from the top until the point of the speed bit sticks out the bottom. Stop, turn the runners over, keeping them together, place them back in the vice and drill the hole from the bottom. Use a round file to smooth out the hole; chamfer the top edge.

12 On the inside face of one runner mark the positions for the four dowels that will join them, 25 mm either side of the steel hole, in the centre and 25 mm in from the opposite end. Drill the four holes in the marked runner 8 mm deep with a 6 mm dowelling drill bit; then,

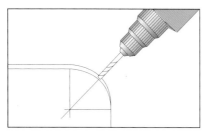

8 Using the pencil line drawn to the inside corner of the square as a guide, drill a hole for the dowel.

9 Cut the dowels to 75 mm long and then cut a slot about a third of the way down each dowel to take the wedge.

using the centre markers from the dowelling kit, transfer the centre marks to the opposing face and drill them to the same depth. Cut four 6 mm dowels, one 22 mm long, one 20 mm long and two 18 mm long. Work adhesive into the holes and onto the dowels. Place the dowels into the holes: short ones at the steel end, the 20 mm one in the centre and the 22 mm one at the other end. The slot will be thinner at the steel end for smaller and thinner knives. Push both pieces together (use a cramp if necessary) and clean any adhesive out of the slot before it dries. Sight along from one end to check the tops are straight. Sand the faces and edges with fine paper.

13 Using a 6 mm dowelling drill bit, drill four 8 mm deep holes along the back of the rear runner, one 35 mm in from each end and one 20 mm each side of centre. Use the centre markers to mark the positions on the backboard, with the top of the runner covering the joint in the backboard. Drill holes 12 mm deep in the backboard. Cut dowels 19 mm

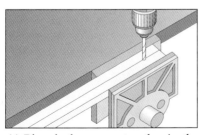

11 Place both runners together in the vice and drill a hole for the steel 50 mm in from the end.

The slot narrows so it holds knives of different widths securely.

long, apply adhesive all along the back of the runner and in the holes and on the dowels. Place the dowels into the holes, and cramp the board and runner together. Using a scraper, clean off as much excess adhesive as possible, then wipe off any residue with a damp cloth. Let the adhesive dry; remove the cramps.

FINISHING
14 Using a sharp chisel as a scraper, remove any dried adhesive. Sand and apply the finish of your choice (see the box on page 21).

15 To fix the rack to the wall, drill four holes approximately 70 mm in from each corner, with a combination drill bit. This puts the screw head below the surface and cuts a hole for a timber plug to be used. If desired, use a plug cutter on a scrap timber piece to cut four plugs and tap them into the holes, with a little adhesive. Allow it to dry and trim off any excess with a sharp chisel. Sand if necessary and touch up the finish.

Wine rack

Diagonal dividers and a front moulding make this very attractive wine rack, which can be used alone for ten bottles, or several can be stacked together or placed side by side to expand capacity.

MATERIALS★				
PART	MATERIAL	LENGTH	WIDTH	No.
Back	12 mm thick MDF	370 mm	295 mm	1
Bottom	12 mm thick MDF	370 mm	303 mm	1
Sides	12 mm thick MDF	330 mm	303 mm	2
Top	12 mm thick MDF	395 mm	303 mm	1
Dividers	12 mm thick MDF	1.2 m	290 mm	2

OTHER: PVA adhesive; 20 mm (¾ in) nails; abrasive paper: medium and fine; 1.2 m of 19 x 19 mm shaped beading; finish of choice

★ Finished size: 330 mm high, 395 mm wide and 320 mm deep. For a note on different types of boards, see page 49.

TOOLS

- Square
- Tape measure
- Steel rule
- Pencil (fine line)
- Circular saw (optional)
- Panel saw
- Jigsaw
- Straight-edge
- Plane (smoothing)
- Vice
- Electric drill
- Drill bit: 12 mm high speed steel (HSS)
- Rubber mallet
- Two G-cramps
- Hammer
- Punch (fine)
- Orbital sander (optional)
- Cork sanding block
- Mitre box or mitre saw
- Dust mask; safety goggles
- Hearing protection

CUTTING OUT

1 Using a panel saw or circular saw, cut the pieces for the box. Plane the edges smooth and check for square.

2 To cut the divider strips, use a circular saw or jigsaw and cramp a straight-edge to the MDF to guide the blade. This ensures an accurate, straight cut, which is important for this project. Do not forget to take into account the distance from the blade to the edge of the base plate. Cut one strip 290 mm wide. Plane

This rack holds ten wine bottles. With its neat, stylish appearance, it will look equally at home in the kitchen or living room.

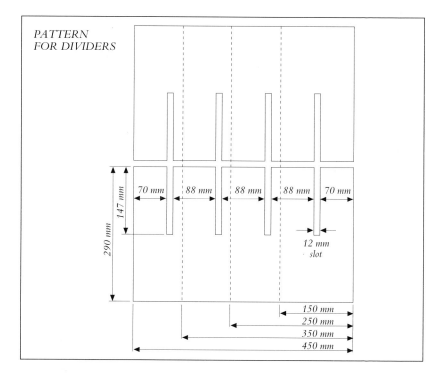

PATTERN FOR DIVIDERS

70 mm | 88 mm | 88 mm | 88 mm | 70 mm

147 mm

290 mm

12 mm
· slot

150 mm
250 mm
350 mm
450 mm

the cut edge on the remaining MDF and cut a second strip 290 mm wide. Mark each face edge.

MAKING THE RACK

3 From the divider strips cut two pieces 150 mm long, two 250 mm long, two 350 mm long and two 450 mm long, using either the circular saw or jigsaw. Take the two 450 mm long strips, put them together with one face edge up and one back edge up, and fasten them into a vice. Using a rule or tape as a

2 Cut three divider strips, using a straight edge cramped to the MDF as a guide for the saw.

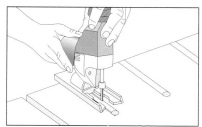

4 Drill a hole at the end of each slot and then use a jigsaw to cut out each of the slots.

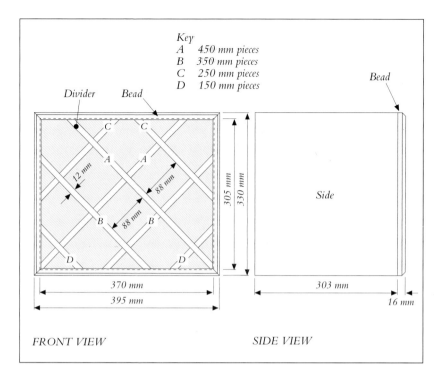

Key
A   450 mm pieces
B   350 mm pieces
C   250 mm pieces
D   150 mm pieces

Divider   Bead

Bead

Divider • C ' C

12 mm   A   A

88 mm

B   88 mm   B

D   D

305 mm   330 mm

Side   Bead

370 mm
395 mm

303 mm
16 mm

FRONT VIEW   SIDE VIEW

guide, mark a point 70 mm in from one end (see the diagram on page 18). Measure 12 mm from the first point and mark, and then mark points at intervals of 88 mm, 12 mm, 88 mm, 12 mm, 88 mm and 12 mm. Square all these marks across the edge of both pieces. Use one piece as a template and transfer the marks to the 350 mm boards. (Place them in the vice, one piece face edge up and one back edge up, and both square at one end.)

4 Using a square, draw lines from the marked edges onto the face, continuing just over halfway across the MDF, 147 mm. Join the ends of

the lines to indicate the slots. Once all the slots are marked, use a 12 mm HSS or speed drill bit to drill a hole at the end of each slot. Using the jigsaw, cut out one slot. Using a small scrap of the same MDF, test the width of the slot: it should be wide enough for the board to slide in easily. Continue cutting out and checking the slots.

5 When all the slots are cut, slide the pieces together to make the rack, according to the diagram above. They should go together without too much force (use a rubber mallet to gently tap them together), as they have to come apart.

6 Place the rack on the work bench, face up and with three junctions closest to you. Measure 35 mm straight down from the outside apex of each junction; mark the nearest timbers on either side. Working on one side, measure 30 mm from the outside apex of the two junctions; mark the nearest timber either side.

7 Place the back onto the rack, lining up the bottom and one side with the marks. Using the back as a guide, continue marking all the way around. Mark every junction, so the rack can be reassembled correctly.

8 Pull the rack apart, tapping it with the mallet if necessary. Use a square, to draw lines on the face from the marked edges at the front, to the back. Adjust the jigsaw base plate to 45 degrees and cramp the first piece down. Cut the lines off so the rack is 1–2 mm smaller than the back and it will slide into the box.

ASSEMBLING THE BOX

9 To assemble the box, glue all the joints and nail them together. First fix the back to the bottom, then the sides and the top. Clean up any excess adhesive, punch the nail heads below the surface and fill the holes.

10 Apply adhesive to all the slots and put the rack back together, making sure the front joints end up as flush as possible. Clean up excess adhesive.

11 Once the adhesive is dry, sand the outside of the box, and the front of the rack, working through the grades from medium to fine. Fill holes or gaps where necessary. Check that the rack fits into the box and, if not, plane off a small amount from the outer edges to help it slide in easily.

12 Paint or stain the rack and the inside of the box, and let them dry. Slide the rack into the box.

13 Sand the beading with fine abrasive paper. Measure the face edges of the box and, using a mitre box or saw, cut four lengths of beading to fit. Glue and nail the beading in place. Let the adhesive dry. Sand and finish the outside of the box.

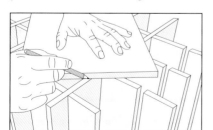

7 Place the back onto the rack and use it as a guide to mark the box shape onto the divisions.

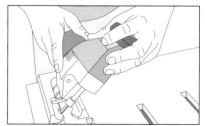

8 Cramp each piece down, adjust the jigsaw base plate and cut along the lines at a 45 degree angle.

FINISHING YOUR PROJECT

PREPARATION

• If timber has received any major bruises, remove the dents by covering them with a wet rag and iron over the rag. The steam and heat will penetrate the timber and swell the grain. This process may need to be repeated a couple of times if the bruising is bad.

• For scratches that go across the grain of timber you may need to use a scraper to remove them properly. Sanding the scratches out is not always successful and can leave a large, unsightly hollow.

• Fill the nail holes and any other gaps in the outer face.

• Give the surface a good sand with fine abrasive paper. If you are using MDF, take care not to sand the faces too hard as this will make them furry, but do work hard on the edges. Use a good quality wood filler to fill bruises or holes that may be visible after finishing.

PAINTING

If you are painting your project, first apply a coat of primer/undercoat so that the timber is well coated. This also makes it easier to sand back to a smooth finish. Apply two coats of the top coat of your choice, remembering to sand between each coat with fine abrasive paper.

If you are using MDF, choose a good quality primer that has been specially formulated for use with MDF.

APPLYING LACQUER OR VARNISH

If you are planning to stain, varnish or lacquer the project, make sure you remove all excess adhesive before applying the finish, or the finish will not penetrate through into the timber and you will be left with white blotches.

First apply a sealer coat of your chosen finish and allow it to dry before sanding it with fine abrasive paper. Apply the final coat using a good quality 75 mm brush for large flat surfaces and always brush in the direction of the grain. Use a well-wetted brush and work from one end to the other with full strokes if possible. Move the brush slowly over the surface and watch the material flow from the brush. In some cases a third coat may be necessary. If so, sand between coats and clean the dust off before applying the final coat.

This fine finish was achieved with several coats of gloss acrylic paint.

Keep your desk tidy and your affairs in order with this attractive and well-designed pigeonhole unit. It includes shelves for paper, slots for envelopes, a cupboard for floppy disks and a drawer for pens and pencils.

Pigeonhole desk storage

The perfect way to store all your desk equipment, this attractive pigeonhole unit includes shelves, a cupboard with door and a drawer. It is relatively simple to make as long as the components are accurately measured and cut.

CUTTING COMPONENTS

1 Using a rule or tape and a square, mark out the components of the unit on the MDF sheets. Be sure to have the stock of the square up against the edge of the sheet when marking parts off the edge. A straight piece of timber can be used to help mark out the larger pieces. Leave about 3–5 mm between each part to allow

MATERIALS★				
PART	MATERIAL	LENGTH	WIDTH	NO.
Top/bottom	12 mm thick MDF	350 mm	235 mm	2
Sides	12 mm thick MDF	370 mm	235 mm	2
Shelves	12 mm thick MDF	334 mm	225 mm	2
Paper slides	6 mm thick MDF	337 mm	224 mm	2
Vertical division	6 mm thick MDF	161 mm	224 mm	2
Cupboard side	12 mm thick MDF	158 mm	225 mm	1
Door	12 mm thick MDF	148 mm	148 mm	1
Drawer front	12 mm thick MDF	324 mm	48 mm	1
Drawer sides	12 mm thick MDF	200 mm	48 mm	2
Drawer bottom	6 mm thick MDF	311 mm	198 mm	1
Drawer back	12 mm thick MDF	310 mm	30 mm	1
Cabinet back	6 mm thick MDF	365 mm	335 mm	1
Drawer runners	6 mm thick MDF	210 mm	11 mm	2

OTHER: Two plastic shelf supports with removable 5 mm steel pins; abrasive paper: three sheets of fine; PVA adhesive; 30 mm (1¼ in) panel pins; 20 mm (¾ in) panel pins; finish of choice; two small handles

★ Finished size: 378 mm high; 350 mm wide and 235 mm deep. For a note on MDF see the box on page 49. For a unit this size you will require two 1200 x 600 mm sheets each of 12 mm and 6 mm thick MDF.

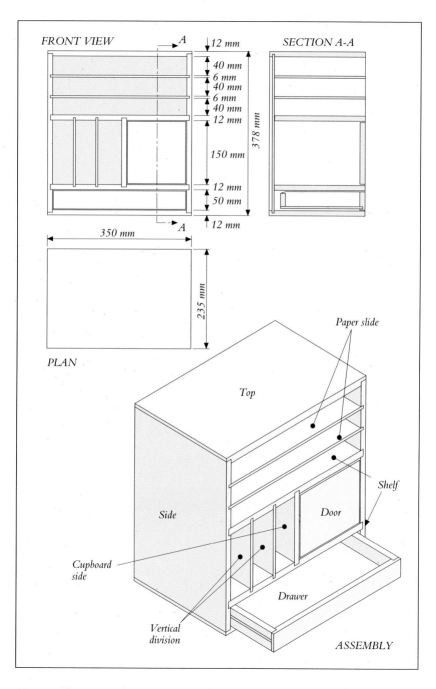

FRONT VIEW

SECTION A-A

12 mm
40 mm
6 mm
40 mm
6 mm
40 mm
12 mm

150 mm

12 mm
50 mm

12 mm

378 mm

350 mm

235 mm

PLAN

Paper slide

Top

Side

Cupboard
side

Vertical
division

Door

Drawer

Shelf

ASSEMBLY

TOOLS

- Folding rule or tape measure
- Combination square
- Pencil
- G-cramps
- Panel saw
- Tenon saw
- Circular saw (optional)
- Vice

- Smoothing plane
- Electric router (optional)
- Router bits: 5 mm and 12 mm straight cutting
- Chisels: 5 mm and 12 mm
- Electric drill
- Drill bit: 5 mm

- Two sash cramps
- Hammer
- Orbital sander (optional)
- Cork sanding block
- Safety goggles
- Hearing protection
- Dust mask

---

for saw cuts. Remember many of the parts will form pairs.

2 Cramp the first sheet of material down to a suitable work surface. Make sure that the area all around the piece is clear. Make the cuts with a panel saw (or circular saw if you have one). Keep to the waste side of the pencil lines and cut straight.

3 Take up the two sides and cramp them together in the vice so that the finished size lines are aligned. Using the smoothing plane, smooth and straighten one long edge back to the lines. Do not go past the lines, and if necessary leave the pieces a little oversize. It is easier to take a small amount of material off at a later stage than it is to cut a new piece and start from scratch.

4 Turn the sides up in the vice so that you can plane the ends back square to the long edge. Check that you are planing straight to the line and that the ends are square to the

long edge and face. Reverse the ends in the vice and plane the other end back to the line. Check with a tape or rule that you have achieved the correct dimensions. Repeat this process for all the components and re-cut any parts that are undersize.

PREPARING THE PARTS

5 Cut the rebates on the top and bottom 12 mm wide and 8 mm deep. If using a router place a 12 mm rebating bit in the router and set the depth of cut to 8 mm. The fence will need to be set to 12 mm. Check that the sides will fit into the rebates neatly with little or no overhang.

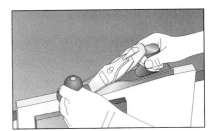

4 Use the smoothing plane to smooth and straighten the edges of all the components, and check them for size.

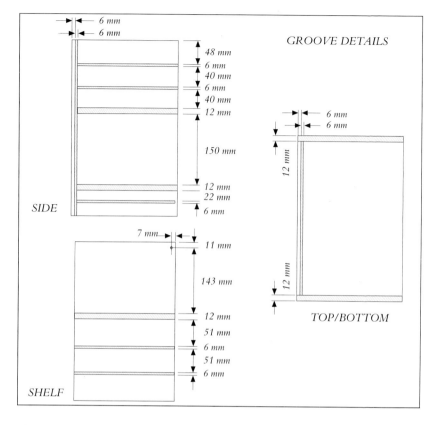

GROOVE DETAILS

6 mm
6 mm

48 mm
6 mm
40 mm
6 mm
40 mm
12 mm

150 mm

12 mm
22 mm
6 mm

SIDE

6 mm
6 mm

12 mm

12 mm

TOP/BOTTOM

7 mm
11 mm

143 mm

12 mm
51 mm
6 mm
51 mm
6 mm

SHELF

6 Take the two drawer sides and cut rebates into the back edges in the same way. Also cut rebates in the drawer front to take the sides.

7 Cut the grooves for the back panel, starting with the top and bottom. Set up the router with the 6 mm straight cutting bit and set the fence so that it is 6 mm away from the cutting edge of the bit and has a cutting depth of 6 mm. Cramp the parts to the work surface so that they will not move, and if you do not have a fence attachment for your router

cramp a fence down over the components. Repeat this step to cut the grooves on the sides. Use a chisel to clean out the grooves if necessary.

8 Cut the grooves in the sides and front of the drawer for the bottom. The settings for the router are the same as in step 7.

9 To ensure the parts are marked out in pairs, align the front edges of the side pieces and mark out the grooves for the paper trays. Similarly, take the two shelves and mark the grooves for

the vertical dividers. Make sure the grooves are in the opposite faces so that the shelves will make a pair. Cut the grooves.

10 Cut the grooves to hold the drawer runners. If using a router, cramp a fence over the top of the sides the correct distance away from the groove. You will have to drop the router into the material to avoid routing through the back edge when you start the cut. Bring the router base against the fence and line the cutter up with the back groove before turning on the router, then lower the router into the material once the cutter has reached maximum speed. This is a delicate operation, so work carefully. Stop the groove 4 mm back from the front edge.

11 Cut the stopped grooves in the drawer side to correspond to the runners. Run them to the front edge.

12 Take the sides and follow the same procedure to cut the 12 mm grooves for the shelves. Then take the shelves and cut a 12 mm groove in the bottom of one and the top of the other as housings for the side of the small cupboard.

13 Take the two shelves and mark the position of the 5 mm pin holes for the door pivots. They should be 143 mm away from the side of the cupboard and set 7 mm back from the front edge. Drill the holes 7 mm deep.

ASSEMBLING

14 Check the pieces fit together, starting with the two shelves and the side of the cupboard. The joints should be a push fit. If the joints are a tight fit, take an off-cut and take a couple of shavings off the face of each side of the off-cut until it slides easily in the groove. Wrap abrasive paper around the off-cut and sand the groove lightly. Try the fit again.

15 Bring the sides into contact with the shelf sub-assembly and push the housing joints home. You may need to use a small sash cramp to pull the joints together fully. Make sure the shelves sit flush with the groove for the back. If the shelves overhang slightly at the front they can be planed back flush later. If the shelves sit back from the front they need to be brought forward so they are flush.

16 Place the bottom in position and hold it in with a cramp. Stand the unit up and slide the back into position. Adjust the back to fit if necessary. If the grooves seem a little tight, adjust them now. Drop the top

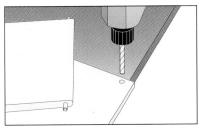

13 Drill holes for the door pins in the shelves, 143 mm from the side of the cupboard and 7 mm from the front.

into position and place a cramp across the unit. Check to see that all the joints fit neatly, that the unit is square by checking the diagonals and that the sides are parallel, not bowed in or out.

17 If the rebated top and bottom do not fit flush with the sides, you may need to set up the router again and make the rebates a fraction wider. Do this first as it will affect the fit of the shelves. If the sides are now bowed out, check that the joints are tight. If they are, adjust the length of the shelves. Plane the ends of both shelves at the same time to keep them the same length and plane only the end away from the door.

18 Check that the paper slides and vertical divisions fit loosely into their grooves. They need to be a loose fit now as the fit will tighten once they are painted. Check that the door fits neatly into the opening with a 1 mm gap all round. Plane the outside (hinged) edge so that it is slightly rounded or it will bind on the side of the cabinet when opened.

19 To assemble the drawer, place the drawer runners in the grooves in the cabinet sides. Next assemble the drawer, without any adhesive or pins at this stage. The drawer is small enough that you should be able to hold it together in your hands. Try slipping the drawer into the cabinet. It should be 1 mm narrower at the back than at the front, allowing it to slip in easily. If it seems to be a little stiff, sand the grooves as described in step 14. If the drawer is still tight you may need to reduce the runner width and thickness slightly.

20 When satisfied with the drawer, take it apart and apply adhesive to the rebates in the drawer front. Bring the sides into position and fasten the joint with 30 mm (1¼ in) panel pins. Slide in the bottom and apply some adhesive to the rear rebates. Turn the drawer over, place a scrap block under the back, place the back in position and fix 20 mm (³/₄ in) panel pins through the bottom and into the back.

21 Take the whole unit apart. Drill the top and bottom edges of the door

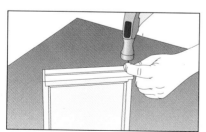

20 Assemble the drawer by applying adhesive to the rebates and nailing the joints with 30 mm (1¹/4 in) panel pins.

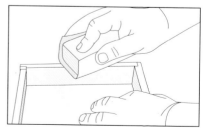

22 Sand the components well, lightly rounding all exposed edges to remove saw marks and repair damage.

for the hinge pins using a 5 mm drill bit. The drilling centres are 142 mm from the closing edge, with a depth of 9 mm.

FINISHING

22 Apply your chosen finish to the parts now (see the box on page 21) as it will be difficult to reach all the surfaces after assembly. First sand all the edges well and then take off the sharp edges. Remove any saw marks and repair any damage. Any holes can be filled with wood filler. Sanding MDF creates very fine dust particles that can cause eye and skin irritation, and so you are well advised to wear a dust mask and goggles.

23 Reassemble the unit, but this time use adhesive. Take the 5 mm steel pins from the shelf supports and discard the shelf supports. When assembling the shelves, insert the pins into the pivot holes and insert the door. Cramp the joint together and drive two 30 mm (1¼ in) panel pins through the shelf into the side of the cupboard. Punch and fill the heads. When the filler dries, sand it back

Neat housing joints are a feature of this pigeonhole unit.

lightly and touch up the marks with the paint.

24 Use 30 mm (1¼ in) panel pins and adhesive to hold the rebate joints together and, if needed, the housing joints. Do not forget to slip in the back panel. Punch and fill all the nail heads. While the filler is drying, lay the unit on its back and check all the joints fit neatly. Apply filler to joints that have gaps. Wait for it to dry; sand with very fine abrasive paper.

25 Using a brush, apply your chosen finish to the exterior and edges (the inside surfaces will be difficult to reach but the finish already applied should be sufficient). Do not forget the drawer and paper slides.

26 Insert the drawer, paper slides and vertical divisions. If the parts do not fit easily, sand the grooves as in step 14 and apply candle wax or soap to the grooves, slides and runners. Fix handles to the door and drawer.

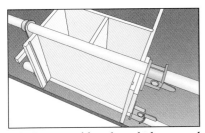

23 Reassemble the shelves and cupboard and then add the sides, cramping the joints together.

Modular display cabinet

Made up of four individual modular units joined together with dowels, this cabinet can be expanded or altered to suit your requirements. Some modules are cupboards with doors, others form open shelves.

MATERIALS★

Part	Material	Length	Width	No.
Sides	15 mm thick MDF	320 mm	250 mm	8
Bottoms	15 mm thick MDF	304 mm	245 mm	4
Rails	15 mm thick MDF	304 mm	226 mm	2
Top	15 mm thick MDF	337 mm	250 mm	1
Shelf	15 mm thick MDF	304 mm	245 mm	1
Door	15 mm thick MDF	302 mm	302 mm	2
Back	15 mm thick MDF	320 mm	325 mm	4
Top back	15 mm thick MDF	320 mm	325 mm	1

OTHER: 2 m of 8 mm dowelling; PVA adhesive; four 110 degree fully concealed cabinet hinges and mounting plates (make sure they are the type that allow the door to be placed inside the cupboard); two handles; eighteen 20 mm (3/4 in) wire nails; finish of choice

★ For this project you will need one 2400 x 1200 mm sheet of MDF board. Finished size of cabinet (four units): 1296 mm high; 336 mm wide; 250 mm deep. Each unit is 320 mm high without top. For a note on MDF see page 49.

TOOLS

- Combination square
- Straight-edge
- Pencil
- Circular saw
- Router (optional)
- Chisel: 25 mm
- Two sash cramps
- Two 400 mm quick-action cramps
- Marking gauge
- Electric drill
- Drill bits: 8 mm, 5 mm, 35 mm end mill
- Smoothing plane
- Hammer
- Screwdriver (cross-head or slotted)
- Dust mask
- Safety goggles
- Hearing protection

The units are made in such a way that they may be stacked up in any configuration. Each has a bottom panel, and a top panel is added only to the topmost unit. The units can also be placed side by side to enlarge the cabinet.

31

PREPARING COMPONENTS

1 Lay the sheet of material across a safe working platform. Mark out the cuts (250 mm apart) to be made along the length of the board using a pencil and a straight-edge. Set up a batten to guide the saw along the cut. It is best to cut the strip a fraction oversize to allow for planing and final sizing at a later stage. Mark out the cross cuts after you have cut each length.

2 With the length firmly secured to the work surface, mark out the cross cuts using a combination square and pencil. If you are using a circular saw, you can mark out and cut as you go.

3 Select the side pieces and place a small cross on what will become the back edge. Using a saw or router with a rebating bit in it, cut the rebates 5 mm wide and 11 mm deep on the back edges.

4 Cramp the sides together in pairs with the front edges flush and the rebates together. With a pencil and square, mark out the positions of the

dowels, on the top and bottom edges, 50 mm in from the front and 55 mm in from the back. Measure carefully as the dowel holes must be positioned absolutely accurately if the components are to fit together.

5 Set the marking gauge to 8 mm as shown in the illustration and mark along each edge to find the centre position at which to drill. Drill the holes to a minimum of 10 mm. Measure 10 mm along the drill bit and place a piece of masking tape there to act as a depth guide when drilling. Be sure to check the drilling pattern for each hole.

6 Take the shelf and rails and cramp them together with their back edges flush. Mark and drill them as for the side pieces but drill the holes to a depth of 30 mm.

7 Take the side pieces of the units with centre shelf or rails and drill dowel holes to correspond to those in the shelf or rails. Cramp the side pieces together in pairs with the inside face up and the rebated edges

4 Cramp the sides together and use a pencil and square to mark a line for the positions of the dowels.

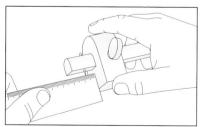

5 Set the marking gauge to 8 mm and mark along the edges to find the centre position for the dowel holes.

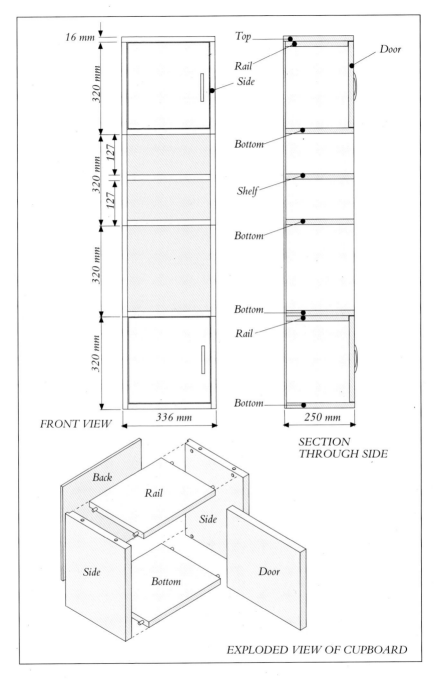

16 mm

320 mm

320 mm

127

127

320 mm

320 mm

FRONT VIEW

336 mm

Top

Rail

Side

Door

Bottom

Shelf

Bottom

Bottom

Rail

Bottom

250 mm

SECTION
THROUGH SIDE

Back

Rail

Side

Side

Bottom

Door

EXPLODED VIEW OF CUPBOARD

together. Mark a line across the centre for the shelf.

ASSEMBLING COMPONENTS

8 With all the holes drilled, check to see all the parts fit together with faces and edges flush. Some of the dowel positions may need to be adjusted by slicing small amounts off the edges of the dowel. When you are satisfied that all parts fit together accurately, decide whether the doors will hang on the left or right side. Place a small mark on the side chosen and take the units apart.

9 Take the sides requiring hinges, and using the template provided with the hinges mark the position of the hinge mounting plates. Be sure to read the mounting instructions very carefully before installing the fittings. It is easier to do this now than when the cupboards are assembled. Fix on the hinge mounting plates and then remove them: they will be fixed back after assembly and painting.

10 Organise the components so that they are in sets, that is with sides, bottom and shelves or top, if applicable, together. Make sure you have a wet rag handy to help remove any excess adhesive that may be squeezed out during clamping. Apply adhesive to the holes and use a pencil to spread it around the hole and remove some of the excess. Add a small bead of adhesive to the edge of the shelves and rails. Spread it with your finger to cover the entire edge.

11 Place the dowels in the holes and gently tap them in with a hammer. Bring the corresponding pieces together and push them into place. If they are a little tight, tap them gently using a hammer and block. Place the cramps centrally near the edge of each side to hold the joints together while the adhesive sets (about 30 minutes). It is wise to use timber off-cuts between the MDF and the cramps to prevent any damage to the surface. Check that the units are square by checking the diagonal measurements to see that they are the same. Adjusting the positions of the cramps slightly can help to square up the unit. Wipe off excess adhesive

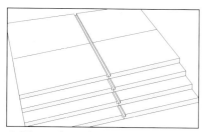

7 Place the side pieces together in pairs with inside face up. Mark a line across the centre for the shelf.

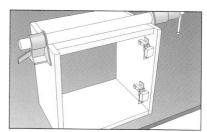

11 Place cramps between the two dowel joints and use timber off-cuts (not shown) to protect the MDF surface.

before it sets, using the wet rag and a chisel to get into the tight corners. Repeat this process for all four modules. If the joints are still loose because of poorly fitting dowels you can place 40 mm (1½ in) panel pins into the joint, punching the nail heads below the surface and filling the holes with filler. Nail a batten across the open end of the three-sided unit to ensure it dries square. Leave the units to dry.

ADDING THE DOORS

12 Take up the doors and check to see that they fit neatly into the cupboard openings. Adjust them with a smoothing plane if necessary. Fit the hinges (see the box at right).

FINISHING

13 Check that the backs fit the cupboards and, if necessary, plane them to fit.

14 Take the doors off the cupboards and prepare all the parts for painting. (It is easier to paint this unit with doors and backs off.) Finish the unit as desired (see the box on page 21).

15 Fit the backs into the side rebates, flush against the bottoms (and rails or shelves if appropriate) and nail in place with 20 mm (¾ in) panel pins.

16 Put the hinges back on the doors and the mounting plates back on the units. Hang and adjust the doors. Fit handles to the doors or touch catches if desired.

FITTING CABINET HINGES

1 Turn the cupboard on its side so that the hinging side is down. Mark a centre line from the mounting plate position to the edge. Bring the door into contact with this closing edge, ensuring it has clearance top and bottom.

2 Transfer the centre line position to the door and square the line in about 30 mm from the edge. Mark the drill centres for the mounting plates on these lines, 21 mm in from the closing edge. Take the end mill and drill the holes 13.5 mm deep. Do not go too deep—a drill stand is essential.

3 Attach the hinges to the doors using the screws supplied or 15 mm (⅝ in) x No.5 gauge screws. Ensure the hinge arm is at right angles to the door edge and attach the door. It is rare for the doors to fit perfectly when you first put them on, and so some adjustments will probably be necessary.

2 Mark out the drill centres for the mounting plates on the doors, 21 mm from the closing edge.

The wicker used in the door panels gives this cupboard an individual appearance but plywood or perforated tin could be used just as effectively.

Cupboard with two doors

This basic cupboard has two doors and stands on a plinth. The doors can be filled with cane, metal or timber to vary the appearance, and the units can be placed side by side to create a larger storage unit.

MATERIALS★

PART	MATERIAL	LENGTH	WIDTH	NO.
Top, bottom	16 mm faced chipboard	730 mm	450 mm	2
Shelf	16 mm faced chipboard	730 mm	444 mm	1
Side pieces	16 mm faced chipboard	650 mm	450 mm	2
Back	6 mm plywood	730 mm	580 mm	1
Kickboard	16 mm chipboard	718 mm	50 mm	1
Door stiles	75 x 19 mm timber	605 mm		4
Door rails	75 x 19 mm timber	235 mm		4

OTHER: 50 mm (2 in) x No.10 chipboard screws; PVA adhesive; nails; one packet 6 mm dowels; 19 mm flat beading; wicker; panel pins; four cabinet hinges; two handles; finish of choice, wood filler

★ This cupboard was made with chipboard but MDF could be used. One sheet will be enough for this project or buy 450 mm panels. Finished size: 655 mm high (including plinth), 750 mm long and 450 mm deep. Timber sizes given are nominal (see page 57).

TOOLS

- Square
- Pencil
- Tape measure
- Tenon saw
- Panel saw or circular saw
- Chisel
- Electric router (optional)
- Router bits: 16 mm straight, 10 mm straight
- Electric drill
- Drill bits (including ones for fixing hinges)
- Countersink bit
- Screwdriver
- Hammer
- Nail punch
- Sash cramps
- Plane
- Cork sanding block
- Dust mask
- Safety goggles
- Hearing protection
- Bradawl

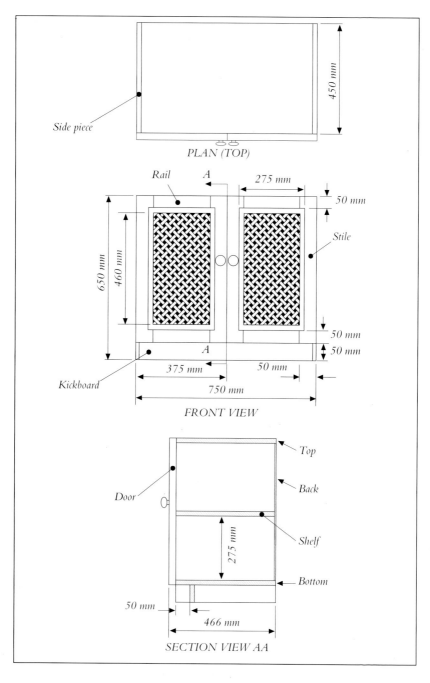

450 mm

Side piece

PLAN (TOP)

Rail   A   275 mm

50 mm

Stile

650 mm   460 mm

50 mm

50 mm

Kickboard   A

375 mm   50 mm

750 mm

FRONT VIEW

Top

Door   Back

275 mm

Shelf

Bottom

50 mm

466 mm

SECTION VIEW AA

MAKING THE CUPBOARD

1 Mark out the parts on the sheet of chipboard, using a square to check that each part is square. Cut them out.

2 Take the two side pieces and on the inside face of each mark the position of the kickboard (50 mm up from the floor end), then make another mark 16 mm above it for the housing for the bottom of the cupboard. Measure up 275 mm from the second line and draw a line for the bottom of the shelf, then draw one 16 mm higher for the top of the shelf. (If you want the shelf higher or lower, adjust the positions of the lines accordingly.) Draw a line 16 mm down from the top edge for the top. When measuring for position, remember to measure from the same side of the board every time. This allows for any irregularities in the shape of the board.

3 Using a saw and chisel, or a router (see box on page 9), cut the grooves for the housing joints 10 mm deep. There will be three grooves in each side, for the top, shelf and bottom.

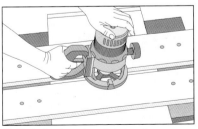

3 Cut the housing joint using a saw and chisel or a router, as here. Place the jig over the lines and cramp.

HINT
To keep track of which face of a piece is which, mark the 'best face' (the one that will be on the outside of the unit) and the 'best edge' (the one that will be seen most). Always measure from this edge (so the mark is not cut off).

4 To accommodate the back panel, make 6 mm rebates in the back edges of the sides, top and bottom. Make sure that the rebate is in the lower part of the top and upper part of the bottom.

5 Drill three 5 mm holes in each groove, one in the centre and one 50–75 mm from each end. Be careful not to drill too close to the edge or the board may split. Countersink these holes from the outside, make pilot holes with a bradawl and then screw the top, the shelf and the bottom to one of the side pieces so that they are flush with the front edge. Repeat the process for the other side.

6 Test the fit of the kickboard in place below the bottom and inset 50 mm from the front edge. If the unit wobbles, plane a little from the bottom edge of the kickboard. Drill two 5 mm holes through one side of the unit, 58 mm in from the front, and 12 mm and 38 mm up from the bottom. Repeat on the other side. Countersink the holes on the outside and screw on the kickboard.

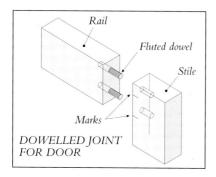

Rail

Fluted dowel

Stile

Marks

DOWELLED JOINT
FOR DOOR

7 Fit the back in place. If it does not fit square, push the unit into shape until it does. Do not trim the backing to fit the unit. Run adhesive around the rebates and along the back edge of the shelf. Position the back and nail in place.

MAKING DOOR FRAMES

8 The stiles and rails of the doors are fixed together with pairs of 6 mm dowels. On the inside edge at the top of each stile, mark the width of the rail. Locate the centre point between this marked line and the top: the dowel holes will be made halfway above and below the centre point (see diagram above). Repeat at the bottom of each stile. For the best results, buy a dowel kit containing a drill, fluted dowels and

centre point markers to transfer the positions of the holes from one piece to the other.

9 Drill the dowel holes, taking care not to make them too deep or too shallow. Allow 5 mm more than the length of the dowel—but do not drill the stile more than 10 mm.

10 Spread adhesive evenly over the dowels and work some into each hole. Insert the dowels into the rail holes.

11 Spread more adhesive over the end grain of the rails, insert the dowels into the stiles and cramp the pieces together. Leave the adhesive to dry as in the manufacturer's specifications. Once the adhesive is set, remove the cramps, plane the joints level and sand the door faces.

12 In the back of the door drill all the holes needed for the hinges (this cannot be done when the cover beading has been fixed to the front). Follow the instructions on the hinge packaging when locating and making the holes.

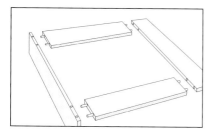

10 Spread adhesive evenly over the dowels and into the holes. Insert the dowels into the holes in the rails.

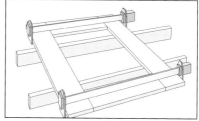

11 Spread adhesive over the end grain of the rails, insert the dowels into the stiles and cramp the pieces together.

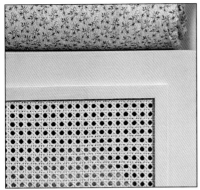

Beading is glued and nailed on to cover the edge of the wicker.

FINISHING

13 Cut the cover beads to length with 45 degree mitres at each corner.

14 Soak the wicker in water for at least an hour, until it has expanded. Give it a shake and hang it up for about 5 minutes. While it is still wet, cut it to size (375 x 600 mm—it needs to be at least 50 mm larger all around than the opening so that you can grasp it to pull it tight). Glue it in position. Use staples or small nails to fix it in place. Cut off the excess wicker for a neat finish.

15 Glue the beading around the edges of the stiles and rails to cover the edges of the wicker, and nail it into place with panel pins. Punch the heads beneath the surface and fill the holes. When the wicker has dried out it should be as taut as a tennis racquet. A gap will appear around the outside of the beading. Fill it with a water-based latex filler.

USING A ROUTER

• Always read the manufacturer's instructions before attempting to operate the router.

• Always use cramps or a vice to hold the work securely so that you have two hands free to operate the router. A fence or batten can also be used to help guide the router.

• Always do a test cut on a scrap piece of material to check the router depth setting before cutting into the components. This will prevent mistakes and improve the quality of your work.

• Wear safety goggles for all routing operations as well as hearing protection and a dust mask.

• When cutting straight grooves and slots use the guide fence supplied or cramp a straight piece of timber to the work and run the base plate of the router firmly along it. Check the positioning carefully before making the cut. Set the router to depth. Run the router across the piece, moving it back and forth so as to remove all the waste.

16 Fix on the hinges (see the box on page 35). Make sure the doors are evenly placed and that they close and open smoothly.

17 Apply the finish of your choice (see the box on page 21). Leave the cupboard to dry. Fix on the door knobs of your choice.

Wall-mounted tool cupboard

The ideal storage place for all your tools, this cupboard is constructed using rebate joints on all corners and housing joints for shelves and divisions. It is hung on the wall by split battens, so it can be lifted off and taken to the job site if required.

CUTTING OUT

1 Decide where you want the shelves and divisions to go in your tool cupboard. The inside of this cupboard has been set up with one main shelf, above which are two vertical dividers with two small shelves attached to the outer side (see

This tool cupboard is easy to make and hang and will keep your tools safely locked away when not needed. All the tools hang in their own place, making them easy to locate and keep in good condition.

photograph above). You can alter this arrangement to suit your tools, but remember to add 12 mm to the desired lengths of the shelves and dividers as each end will be set 6 mm into a housing joint.

2 Cut all material to size using a hand saw or jigsaw. Be careful to cut square and straight. For greater accuracy, use a

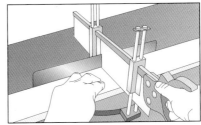

2 Cut all material to size. Using a mitre saw such as this ensures greater accuracy when cutting.

TOOLS

- Panel saw
- Tenon saw
- Jigsaw (optional)
- Coping saw (optional)
- Mitre saw (optional)
- Circular saw (optional)
- Tape measure
- Pencil

- Square
- Electric router (optional)
- Router bit: 18 mm straight
- Chisel: 20 mm
- Electric drill
- Drill bits: various sizes
- Hammer
- Nail punch

- Block plane
- Electric sander (optional)
- Cork sanding block
- Screwdriver (to suit hinges)
- Dust mask
- Safety goggles
- Hearing protection

mitre saw or guide a jigsaw along a straight timber batten. You may need to use a block plane to square the ends and a square to check for accuracy. Stack each section together to ensure all parts are cut out correctly.

CUTTING THE JOINTS

3 Select one side piece and use a tenon saw or router with a 20 mm bit guided along a straight piece of timber to cut a rebate 12 mm deep on the inside face at either end. Repeat for other sides.

4 Select the two sides for the centre section. Place them side by side on a flat surface and set out the housing joints for the shelves. For the main shelf, measure up from the bottom 300 mm and square a line across both pieces at this point. Measure up a further 22 mm (or the thickness of the shelf material) and draw a parallel line. These two lines represent the width of the housing joint.

5 Carefully cut out the housing groove 6 mm deep (or one-third of the thickness of the timber using the router or a tenon saw and chisel). Then repeat this process on the other side piece.

6 Set out the positions for the small shelves at even spaces (or to suit your

3 If using a router to make the end rebates, fix a straight piece of timber to the board at right angles.

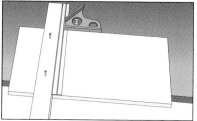

5 To make the housing grooves with a router, first nail (or clamp) a piece of timber to the board as a guide.

MATERIALS★

PART	MATERIAL	LENGTH	NO.
Side (centre/doors)	25 x 150 mm pine PAR	900 mm	6
Centre top/bottom	25 x 150 mm pine PAR	888 mm	2
Door top/bottom	25 x 150 mm pine PAR	435 mm	4
Divider	25 x 150 mm pine PAR	558 mm	2
Main shelf	25 x 150 mm pine PAR	876 mm	1
Small shelf	25 x 150 mm pine PAR	176 mm	4
Door shelf	25 x 75 mm pine PAR	423 mm	2
Split battens	25 x 75 mm pine PAR	900 mm	2
Centre back	6 mm plywood	900 x 900 mm	1
Door back	6 mm plywood	900 x 450 mm	2

OTHER: PVA adhesive; 40 mm (1½ in) lost-head nails; 25 mm (1 in) panel pins; abrasive paper: medium; two 900 mm piano hinges; two 50 mm barrel bolts; hasp and staple lock; 25 mm (1 in) x No.6 gauge round-head screws; 50 mm (2 in) x No.8 gauge countersunk screws; 6 x 6 mm beading; tool mounting clips

★ With doors closed the cupboard measures 900 mm high, 900 mm wide and 276 mm deep. Timber sizes given are nominal (see the box on page 57).

needs). With the two side pieces placed side by side as before, transfer the position from one to the other. Remove one of the side pieces and place a divider in its place, with the top of the divider 12 mm down from the top of the side piece (as it will be set into the top piece). Square the small shelf marks across onto the divider and repeat with the other side and divider. Cut the housings using a saw and chisel, or with a router.

7 Set out the housing joints in the top and the main shelf by placing them side by side on a flat surface and measuring 170 mm in from each end. Square a line across at this point and another a further 22 mm on (the thickness of the material). Cut the housing joints.

THE DOOR SHELVES

8 To make the slotted shelves to hold screwdrivers, files or chisels, drill holes the required distance apart (about 50 mm) into the centre of the door shelves and cut slots from the holes to the front edge with a tenon saw. The holes and slots may vary in size to suit the tools.

9 Take the two sides of one door and set out stopped housing joints for the slotted shelves, measuring up the required distance from the bottom,

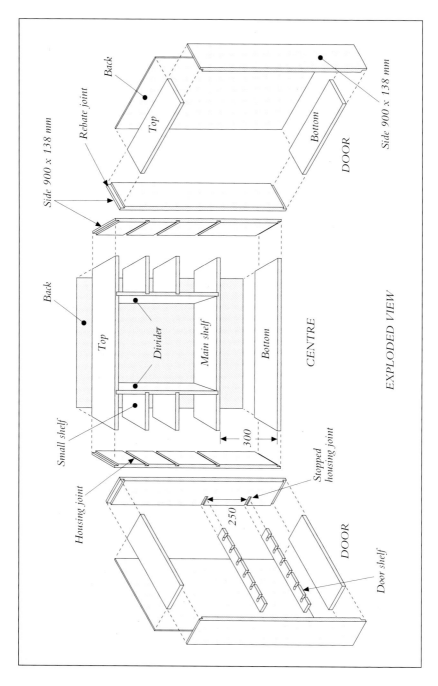

EXPLODED VIEW

and allowing enough space between (about 250 mm) to get the tools in and out. Lay the two side pieces side by side. Measure across from the back edge the width of the shelves and mark a line parallel to this edge where the housing will stop. Mark all four stopped housing joints, making sure the sides make a pair (one left-handed and one right-handed). Cut out the housings, being careful not to go past the stopped end. Square the ends of the housings with a chisel and check the fit of each shelf.

THE CUPBOARD

10 To assemble the cupboard, work on one housing joint at a time, applying adhesive and then nailing through the joint using 40 mm (1½ in) lost-head nails. Begin with the centre section: take one divider and fix one small shelf, then the other. Repeat for the other divider. Fix the dividers to the main shelf and top.

11 Apply adhesive to the housing joints and the top rebate joint on one side piece. Fit the side piece to the shelf assembly and nail through the outside into the end of each shelf. Then nail through the top piece into the rebate joint. Fix the other side to the unit in the same way. Stand the unit on its top, and glue and nail the bottom in place by nailing through the timber into the rebate joint.

12 Assemble the doors using the same method.

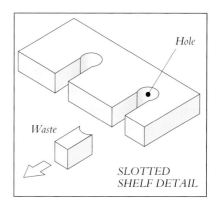

Hole

Waste

SLOTTED SHELF DETAIL

13 Lay the centre section on a flat surface and flush up any of the joints using a smoothing plane. Check the section is square by measuring the diagonals. If necessary, apply light pressure to the longer diagonal until it is square. Apply adhesive to the edge and place the plywood back in position. Fix it using 25 mm (1 in) panel pins approximately 40–50 mm apart, nailing to all sides, shelves, dividers, top and bottom. Neaten the edges by planing and sanding the whole job. Repeat this on the two doors.

THE DOORS

14 Although the tools to go on the doors are lightweight, the doors will still carry a fair amount of weight, so piano hinges are best, although butt hinges of reasonably good quality will do. The leaf of the piano hinge is 12 mm wide and 1 mm thick. Run a rebate down the full length of the side pieces of the cupboard and on the hinge side of the doors (the 12 mm will be on the edge of these pieces). Fix the hinge in position

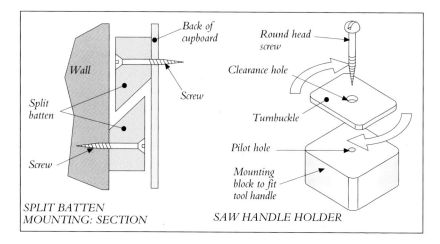

**SPLIT BATTEN
MOUNTING: SECTION**

SAW HANDLE HOLDER

with the screws provided (usually 16 mm (⅝ in) x No.4 gauge), placing one in the top and bottom and one in the centre on each side. Check the operation of the door, adjust as required and then fix all the screws.

15 To hold the door shut, use barrel bolts on the inside of one

door, top and bottom. On the other door fit a lock or a hasp and staple with a padlock.

TOOL MOUNTINGS
16 For small tools, use commercially available tool mounting clips or hooks. To hang the saws and level, glue on blocks of timber cut to the inside shape of the handle and attach turnbuckles made from scrap ply or timber and fixed to the handle blocks with 25 mm (1 in) x No.6 gauge round-head screws (see diagram above). To hold the squares use pieces of timber with a rebate in the back edge the size of the blade.

17 To prevent tools falling off the shelves, pin small beading (6 x 6 mm) along each shelf. Do not glue it as you may need to move it later. Fix a small piece of beading across the shelf where the planes will fit. This will help protect the blade from damage by keeping the edge up off the shelf.

POSITIONING THE TOOL
CUPBOARD

When deciding where to hang your cupboard, consider how easy it will be to get the tools in and out. There should be enough clearance so that the doors will open at least to a right angle. The cupboard should not be placed so high that you cannot reach the tools or so low that you cannot place a workbench under it. Placing it so that the bottom is about 1.2 m off the floor or 300 mm above your workbench is ideal.

FIXING TO THE WALL

18 To make the split battens, set the circular saw at a 45 degree angle and rip a 900 mm piece of 75 x 25 mm timber down the centre of the face to produce two pieces of timber the same width with a bevel on one edge. Make two sets of battens, one to go at the top and one at the bottom of the cupboard. Drill clearance holes through them corresponding to the centres of the unit sides and (for the top batten only) the two dividers.

19 Lay the unit face down and position the battens approximately 75 mm in from the top and bottom, ensuring that the bevel edge of each batten is on the bottom and the wide face is on the outside. Drill pilot holes through the clearance holes in the battens into the cupboard and fix using 50 mm (2 in) x No.8 gauge screws.

20 Decide where you will hang the cupboard and the distance from the bottom of the cupboard to the floor (see the box on page 48). Place the remaining half of each batten against the ones fixed to the cupboard. Measure the distance up from the bottom of the cupboard to the lower edge of each pair of battens. Add this measurement to the distance from the bottom of the cupboard to the floor and mark the positions on the wall. Fix the battens to the wall with the bevelled side upwards, using at least three 50 mm (2 in) x No.8 gauge screws for each and ensuring the battens are level and in line with

each other. If you are fixing the cupboard to a framed wall, make sure the screws have solid fixing into the frame. If you are fixing it to a masonry wall, use plastic wall plugs or other suitable fixings.

21 Lift the tool cupboard onto the wall just above the battens and slide it down until it rests neatly and firmly on the battens.

22 If desired, apply a finish of your choice (see the box on page 21).

MANUFACTURED BOARDS

Two types of manufactured boards are commonly used, chipboard and MDF.
• Chipboard, made from timber chips bonded together, is rarely used in its raw state but it also comes with a melamine or timber veneer. To give a good finish, exposed edges need to be covered with a matching edging material.
• MDF (medium density fibreboard) is an ideal material for building furniture as you can use a plane and router on it and it does not need finishing, although it will take a surface treatment if desired. However, it does contain chemicals that can cause skin problems in some people. Always work out of the sun. Wear gloves if you have sensitive skin and protect your eyes, nose, mouth and lungs from the dust.

Bright colours and hard-wearing paints make this storage unit ideal for a child's bedroom but painted in more subtle shades it would look just as useful anywhere in the house.

Shelves with storage boxes

These handy little boxes not only look great but provide excellent storage space. The hand holes in the ends of each box make it easy to slide them in and out, and the shelf unit is conveniently at standard table height.

CUTTING OUT

1 Using a pencil and measuring tape, mark out all the parts on the MDF sheet, allowing enough clearance between each piece for the cut. Double check that every part has been drawn.

2 Cut out the pieces using either a panel or circular saw. Trim your pieces to size using a smoothing plane or, for a better finish, use a router (running it along a straight edge). Use a square to check for accuracy on all edges and faces. As

MATERIALS★				
PART	MATERIAL	LENGTH	WIDTH	NO.
Unit top	15 mm thick MDF	790 mm	400 mm	2
Unit end	15 mm thick MDF	736 mm	380 mm	2
Unit divider	15 mm thick MDF	660 mm	380 mm	1
Unit bottom	15 mm thick MDF	730 mm	380 mm	1
Unit shelves	15 mm thick MDF	361 mm	380 mm	2
Kickboard	15 mm thick MDF	720 mm	66 mm	1
Unit back	6 mm thick MDF	744 mm	685 mm	1
Box front/back	9 mm thick MDF	350 mm	250 mm	8
Box side	9 mm thick MDF	340 mm	250 mm	8
Box bottom	6 mm thick MDF	340 mm	340 mm	4

OTHER: 50 mm (2 in) lost-head nails; 30 mm (1¹/₄ in) lost-head nails; 20 mm (³/₄ in) wire nails; six 50 mm (2 in) x No.8 gauge cross-head screws; six 25 mm (1 in) x No.8 gauge cross-head screws; four 75 mm (3 in) x No.8 gauge cross-head screws; abrasive paper: three sheets each of medium and fine; PVA adhesive; craft adhesive; filler; 100 x 1200 mm piece of felt; finish of choice

★ One sheet of each thickness of MDF will make this project. For a note on MDF see the box on page 49. Finished size: 766 mm high, 790 mm wide, 400 mm deep. Boxes are 250 mm high, 350 mm wide and 350 mm deep.

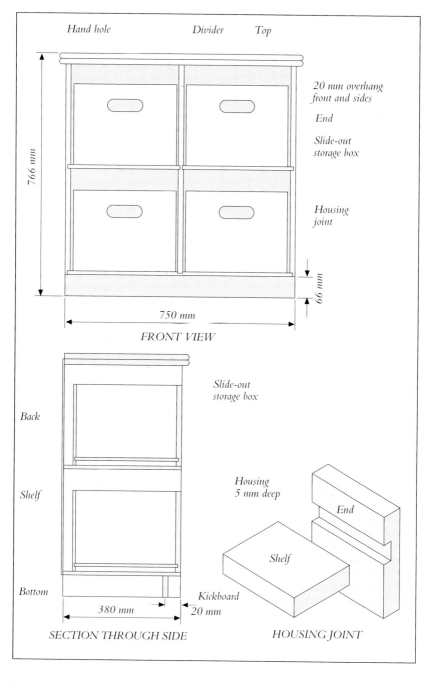

Hand hole   Divider   Top

20 mm overhang
front and sides

End

Slide-out
storage box

Housing
joint

766 mm

66 mm

750 mm

FRONT VIEW

Slide-out
storage box

Back

Shelf

Housing
5 mm deep

End

Shelf

Bottom

Kickboard
20 mm

380 mm

SECTION THROUGH SIDE

HOUSING JOINT

TOOLS		
• Soft pencil	• Large square	• Screwdriver (Pozidriv No. 2)
• Tape measure	• Electric router (optional)	• Chisel: 25 mm (optional)
• Panel or circular saw	• Router bits: 16 mm straight, 10 mm straight and 6 mm rounding	• Circular saw (optional)
• Tenon saw		• Dust mask
• Electric drill: HSS bit		
• Smoothing plane	• Electric sander (optional)	• Safety goggles
• Chisel	• Cork sanding block	• Hearing protection
• Marking gauge (optional)	• Hammer	
• Straight-edge	• Nail punch	

you cut each piece, use a soft pencil to number or label each part on the inside face for easy identification.

CUTTING HOUSING JOINTS

3 Take the unit ends and decide which of them will be the left-hand end and which the right-hand end. On the inside face of each piece, measure up 66 mm from the bottom and mark a line parallel to the bottom edge with a soft pencil. This line indicates the position where the kickboard will be located.

4 Measure up 15 mm (the thickness of the sheet material) from the first pencil line and draw another parallel line representing the bottom of the unit. Then measure the distance to the top and divide by two in order to determine the position of the shelf. Mark this position with a parallel line. To set out the housing joint for the shelf, measure 7.5 mm either side of this line, drawing a parallel line each time.

5 Lay one marked-out end piece on a flat surface and place the divider beside it so the top edges are aligned. Using a large square, transfer the set out lines for the shelf from the end piece to the division. Turn the division over and repeat on the other side. If you do not have a large square, use a tape measure and straight-edge.

6 Lay the unit bottom on a flat surface with the inside face upward and measure the length. Divide this by two to find the centre; square a line across the face. Measure 7.5 mm either side and draw two parallel lines to mark the housing joint.

7 Cut out the housing joints 5 mm deep using a tenon saw and chisel, or a router and 15 mm straight bit (see the box on page 9).

ASSEMBLING THE SHELVES

8 Lay the two end pieces side by side on a flat surface, and check that one is for the left end and one for the

---

CUTTING THE MATERIAL

If you do not want to cut the material yourself, you may take advantage of the cut-to-size service offered by some companies. Check your local telephone directory for fibreboard suppliers who offer this service.

---

right. On the bottom of each piece, measure back 20 mm from the front edge and square a line up to the bottom of the housing for the position of the kickboard.

9 Using your jigsaw or panel saw, remove this 66 x 20 mm corner from the end pieces by cutting along the line and bottom edge of the housing.

10 Round off the front and end edges of the two top pieces, using a plane and abrasive paper or a router with a 6 mm rounding bit inserted. Don't round the back edge.

11 Smooth all edges and faces with medium abrasive paper.

12 To attach the shelf, first apply PVA adhesive to the housing joints on one end piece. On a flat surface, stand this side and one shelf on their back edges. Bring the shelf into the glued joint, ensuring it fits snugly on the bottom of the housing and that the front edges are flush. At least 40 mm in from the front and back edges, drive a 30 mm (1¼ in) lost-head nail through the bottom of the

shelf into the housing at an angle so that the nail will not come through the outside. Punch the nail below the surface. Repeat this process when attaching the bottom to the end piece, ensuring that the housing joint for the divider is facing upwards.

13 Apply adhesive to the housing joint on the bottom piece and the divider. Place the divider into the housing and then fit the shelf into the housing in the divider, ensuring all joints fit well. Using 50 mm (2 in) lost-head nails, nail through the bottom into the end of the divider. Nail through the shelf housing in the divider into the end of the shelf. Glue and skew nail, with 30 mm (1¼ in) lost-head nails, the remaining shelf and end in the correct position.

14 Stand the unit upright and lay one top piece on the unit with a 20 mm overhang on each end and the front. Check the divider and end pieces are parallel. Drill through the top into the ends and divider; secure the top to each piece with 50 mm (2 in) x No.8 gauge screws. Lay the second top piece over the first, ensuring it lines up on all edges. Secure the two tops together by drilling and screwing from underneath using 25 mm (1 in) x No. 8 gauge screws. We used three across the front and three across the back approximately 25 mm in from each upright piece.

15 To attach the kickboard to the unit, drill four 4 mm holes through

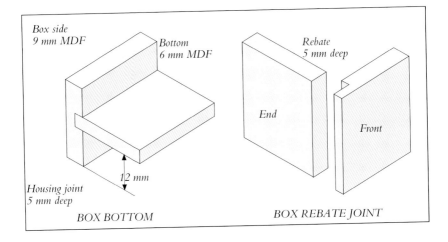

Box side
9 mm MDF

Bottom
6 mm MDF

Rebate
5 mm deep

End

Front

12 mm

Housing joint
5 mm deep

BOX BOTTOM

BOX REBATE JOINT

the bottom edge of the kickboard, one approximately 50 mm from each end and two evenly spaced between. Lay the unit on its back and place the kickboard in position, 5 mm back from the front edge of the side pieces. Fix with 75 mm (3 in) screws. Glue and nail a small block of scrap timber 50 mm long to the ends behind the kickboard for added strength.

16 Lay the unit down on its face on a flat surface. Measure and check the diagonals to ensure that the unit is square. Place the back in position and fix it to all edges of the unit, including the divider and shelves. Use 20 mm (¾ in) wire nails and set them approximately 40–50 mm apart.

CUTTING OUT THE BOXES

17 Select the front and back pieces for the boxes. Using a router with 9 mm straight bit, or a circular or tenon saw and chisel, cut a rebate 5 mm deep and 9 mm wide into the inside face of both short edges.

18 Cut the grooves to hold the

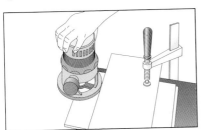

17 Using a router (or saw and chisel), cut a rebate 5 mm deep and 10 mm wide into both ends.

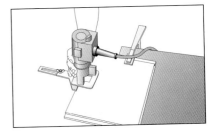

18 Cut the grooves for the bottom, first testing on a piece of scrap and checking the fit.

bottom 5 mm deep on the inside faces of all the front, back and side pieces. If using a router insert a 6 mm bit and set the guide fence 12 mm from the edge of the cutter.

19 To make the hand holes, select one front piece and mark the centre on the top edge. Measure 50 mm to the left of this point and square a line across the face. Repeat this to the right of the centre point. Measure 40 mm down the face on these lines and mark. Centre an electric drill with an HSS bit on each point and drill through. Join the holes together with lines at the top and bottom edge to create a long oval shape. Cut along this line with the jigsaw. Smooth the edges of the hole with abrasive paper. Repeat for all front and back pieces.

ASSEMBLING THE BOXES

20 Each box consists of two sides, a front, a back and a bottom. Using one side and a front, apply adhesive to the rebate joint and assemble the joint by placing the side piece into the rebate. Using 30 mm (1¼ in) lost-head nails,

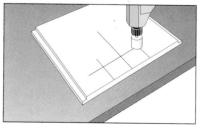

19 Centre electric drill with HSS bit on the desired point and drill through the piece to start the hand hole.

Felt is glued to the base of the box sides to act as runners.

nail through the side piece into the rebate joint, ensuring the grooves line up so the bottom will fit easily.

21 Repeat this process and attach the back to the remaining side. Select one half of the box and fit the bottom into the groove. Apply adhesive to the rebate joints and attach the remaining half of the box. Nail the rebate joints together.

22 Punch all nails to ensure that the joints fit tightly. Before the adhesive sets, check that the box is square by measuring the diagonals. If necessary, apply light pressure to the longer diagonal until it is square. Fill all nail holes with filler and sand the edges using medium grade abrasive paper, ensuring that all joints are flush.

FINISHING

23 Apply the finish of your choice (see box on page 21). Leave to dry.

24 Use craft adhesive to glue 10 mm wide strips of felt to the base of the box sides. This will help the boxes

TIMBER

SOFTWOOD OR HARDWOOD?

Timber is classified as either softwood or hardwood, but this classification depends not on the relative hardness or density of the timber, but on the type of tree it comes from. For example, balsa, a softish timber used to make model aeroplanes and other lightweight models, is actually a hardwood. Hardwoods are mostly from deciduous trees that lose their leaves in winter; softwoods are from conifers with needle-like leaves.

For most of the projects in this book you can choose either a softwood or a hardwood. The main determining factors will be cost, availability and suitability for the particular project.

TIMBER CONDITIONS

Timber is sold in three conditions:
• sawn or rough sawn: brought to a specific (nominal) size by band saw
• planed all round (PAR)
• moulded: processed to a specific profile for architraves, window sills, skirting boards and so on

Planed timber is sold using the same nominal dimensions as sawn timber, for example 100 x 50 mm, but the surfaces have all been machined down to a flat, even width and thickness so that the '100 x 50 mm' timber is actually between 95 x 45 mm and 97 x 47 mm. The chart below shows the maximum sizes for seasoned planed timber sold in nominal sizes. Some suppliers now label wood with its 'actual' dimensions. Always check sizes before use.

Moulded timbers are also ordered by their nominal sizes. Their finished sizes will generally compare with those given in the chart for planed timber, but check them carefully at the timber yard as there will be many variations.

Timber is sold in standard lengths, beginning at 1.8 m and increasing by 300 mm to 2.1 m, 2.4 m and so on. Short lengths and off-cuts are also usually available.

Sawn (nominal) size (mm)	Maximum after planing (mm)
10	7
12	9
19	16
25	22
32	29
38	35
50	47
75	72
100	97
125	122
150	147
175	172
200	197
225	222
250	247
300	297

Boxes with lids and castors

These boxes are simple to make and provide a practical storage option. The castors on the boxes make them easy to handle, and the lids ensure they are reasonably dustproof. The fronts, backs and sides are held together with rebated joints and the bottoms are fitted into grooves.

MATERIALS★				
PART	MATERIAL	LENGTH	WIDTH	NO.
Fronts/backs	15 mm thick MDF	350 mm	250 mm	8
Sides	15 mm thick MDF	600 mm	250 mm	8
Bottoms	9 mm thick MDF	600 mm	338 mm	4
Lids	9 mm thick MDF	600 mm	338 mm	4
Locating battens	12 x 12 mm timber		326 mm	8

OTHER: Abrasive paper: three sheets each of medium and fine, and two sheets of very fine; PVA adhesive; 30 mm (1¼ in) lost-head nails; finish of choice; four 50 mm castors per box; 12 mm (½ in) x No.6 gauge screws

★ One sheet of each thickness of board will make four boxes 270 mm high, 350 mm wide and 612 mm deep. The size of these boxes may need to be adjusted to fit under your particular bed. For a note on MDF see page 49.

TOOLS

- Tape measure
- Pencil
- Panel saw
- Jigsaw
- Tenon saw
- Circular saw (optional)
- Straight-edge
- Smoothing plane
- Electric router (optional)

- Router bits: 9 mm straight and 6 mm rounding
- Chisel: 25 mm
- Square
- Marking gauge (optional)
- Hammer
- Nail punch
- Cork sanding block
- Electric drill

- Drill bits: 3 mm high speed steel (HSS) bit
- Screwdriver (to suit castors)
- Dust mask
- Safety goggles
- Hearing protection

These practical and smart storage boxes will have plenty of use as they slide in and out under the bed. Without the castors, they could be stacked for more permanent storage.

CUTTING THE MATERIAL

1 Mark out all the parts on the material, ensuring each part is there and on the right thickness of board. Allow enough clearance between the various pieces to be able to cut them out easily.

2 Cut out the pieces using either a panel saw or jigsaw. If preferred, you can use a circular saw, with a straight-edge to ensure the cuts remain straight. Trim all the pieces to size with a smoothing plane. Use the square to check that all edges and faces are square.

3 Take one front piece and measure up 40 mm from the bottom edge. Mark a parallel line the full length of the material. This is where the bottom of the box will be inserted, allowing 10 mm clearance off the floor for the castor (adjust this distance if you are using castors other than 50 mm). Using a saw and chisel or a router with 9 mm bit (see the box on page 9), cut a 9 mm deep groove the full length of the material. Fit one of the bottom pieces into this

groove and ensure that it fits neatly. Complete the bottom groove on the inside face of all the front, back and side pieces.

4 On the front and back pieces cut rebates in the inside face (the same side as the groove) of both ends. Make the rebate 9 mm deep and 15 mm wide and cut them using the router, or a circular saw or tenon saw and chisel.

5 Select the box lids and round all four corners and the top edges to a 6 mm radius, using the smoothing plane and some fine abrasive paper, or using the router with a 6 mm rounding bit inserted.

MAKING HAND HOLES

6 To make a hand hole, select the front piece of one box and mark the centre on the top edge. Measure 50 mm to the left of this point and square a line across the face. Repeat this to the right of the centre point. Measure 40 mm down the face on these lines and place a mark. Centre the electric drill with high speed bit

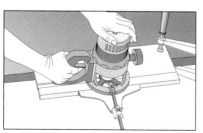

3 To make the groove for the bottom using a router, set the fence guide to 40 mm and cut the full length.

4 Cut a rebate 9 mm deep by 15 mm wide in both ends of the inside face of the front and back pieces.

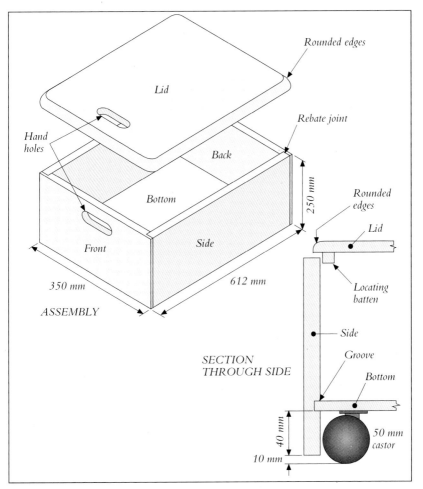

Rounded edges

Lid

Rebate joint

Hand holes

Back

250 mm

Rounded edges

Lid

Bottom

Locating batten

Front

Side

Side

350 mm

612 mm

Groove

ASSEMBLY

Bottom

SECTION
THROUGH SIDE

50 mm
castor

40 mm

10 mm

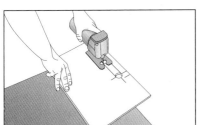

6 To make a hand hole, drill two holes with the electric drill and join them together with the jigsaw.

on each of these points and drill through the piece. Join the drill holes by drawing lines across at the top and bottom edges, creating a long oval shape. Cut along the lines with the jigsaw. Smooth the edges of the hole with abrasive paper. Make a hole in each front piece and each lid, positioning the holes in the lids in the same way.

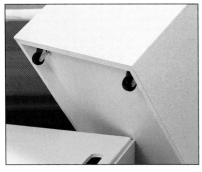

Castors raise the box off the floor.

ASSEMBLING THE BOX

7 Take one side and a front, apply adhesive to the rebate joint and assemble the joint by placing the side piece into the rebate. Using 30 mm (1¼ in) lost-head nails, nail through the side piece into the rebate joint, ensuring that the grooves in both pieces are lined up so that the bottom will fit easily.

8 Repeat this process to attach the back to the remaining side. Select one half of the box and fit the

---

POWER TOOLS

• Power tools can be used to make some of the heavier work in these projects much easier, but they are not essential. All the projects can be made using only traditional hand tools if you prefer or if you do not have access to the power tool specified.

• When using power tools, always wear safety goggles, hearing protection and a dust mask.

---

bottom into the groove. Apply adhesive to the rebate joints and attach the remaining half of the box. Nail the rebate joints together.

9 Punch all nails to ensure that the joints fit tightly. Before the adhesive sets, check that the box is square by measuring the diagonals. If necessary, apply light pressure to the longer diagonal until it is square.

MAKING THE LID

10 Take two 12 x 12 mm battens per lid and glue and nail them to the underside of each lid, 12 mm in from the front and back edges respectively and positioned so they finish 12 mm in from the sides. The battens should fit neatly inside the box when the lid is in position to prevent it sliding off.

FINISHING

11 Wearing a dust mask, sand all edges well using medium grade abrasive paper. Apply the finish of your choice (see the box on page 21).

12 On the underside of the box, measure in 40 mm from each side at the corner. Mark this with a pencil and drill a 3 mm pilot hole. This will be the outside corner of the castor mounting plate and allow sufficient room for the castor wheel to swivel. Attach the castor with a 12 mm (1½ in) x No.6 gauge screw, ensuring the plate is parallel to the outside edge of the box. Drill the remaining pilot holes and fix the screws. Fix the remaining castors in the same manner.

Tools for making storage projects

Some of the most useful tools for making storage projects are shown below. Build up your tool kit gradually—most of the tools can be purchased from your local hardware store.

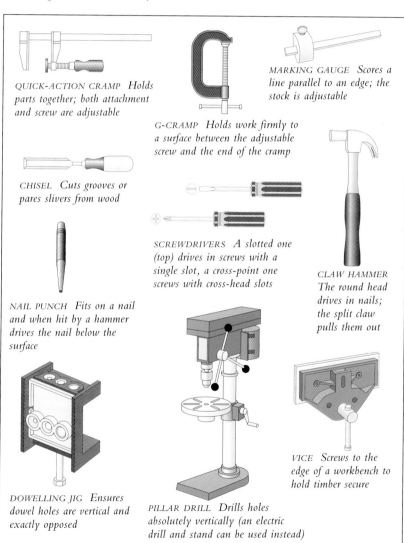

QUICK-ACTION CRAMP Holds parts together; both attachment and screw are adjustable

MARKING GAUGE Scores a line parallel to an edge; the stock is adjustable

G-CRAMP Holds work firmly to a surface between the adjustable screw and the end of the cramp

CHISEL Cuts grooves or pares slivers from wood

SCREWDRIVERS A slotted one (top) drives in screws with a single slot, a cross-point one screws with cross-head slots

CLAW HAMMER The round head drives in nails; the split claw pulls them out

NAIL PUNCH Fits on a nail and when hit by a hammer drives the nail below the surface

DOWELLING JIG Ensures dowel holes are vertical and exactly opposed

PILLAR DRILL Drills holes absolutely vertically (an electric drill and stand can be used instead)

VICE Screws to the edge of a workbench to hold timber secure

Index

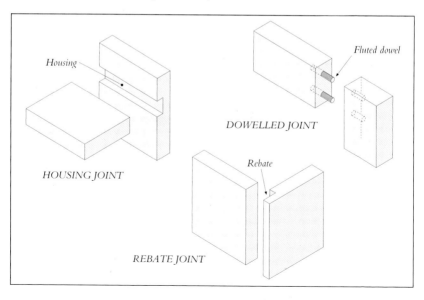

Housing

DOWELLED JOINT

Fluted dowel

HOUSING JOINT

Rebate

REBATE JOINT